# NURSERY
## *Poems & Prayers*

*featuring the art of*
## BESSIE PEASE GUTMANN

Publishers · GROSSET & DUNLAP · New York
A member of The Putnam & Grosset Book Group

# Poems and Prayers in Alphabetical Order

# GOOD MORNING, MERRY SUNSHINE

Good morning, merry sunshine,
How did you wake so soon?
You've scared the little stars away,
And shined away the moon;
I saw you go to sleep last night,
Before I ceased my playing.
How did you get 'way over here,
And where have you been staying?

I never go to sleep, dear;
I just go round to see
My little children of the East
Who rise and watch for me.
I waken all the birds and bees,
And flowers on the way,
And last of all the little child
Who stayed out late to play.

# MONDAY'S CHILD

Monday's child is fair of face,
Tuesday's child is full of grace,
Wednesday's child is full of woe,
Thursday's child has far to go,
Friday's child is loving and giving,
Saturday's child works hard for a living,
And the child that's born on the Sabbath day
Is fair and wise and good and gay.

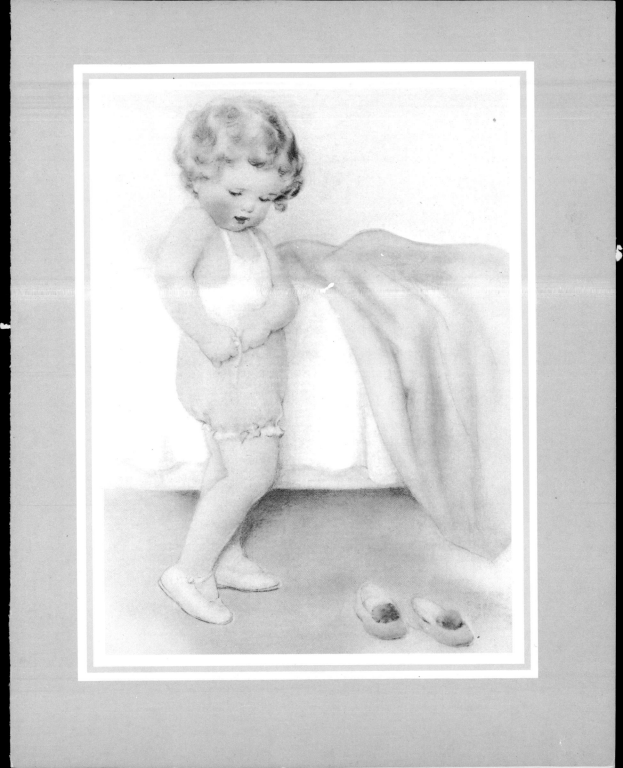

# PAT-A-CAKE

Pat-a-cake, pat-a-cake, baker's man,
Bake me a cake as fast as you can;
Pat it and prick it, and mark it with a B,
And put it in the oven for Baby and me.


# PEASE PORRIDGE HOT

Pease porridge hot, pease porridge cold,
Pease porridge in the pot, nine days old.
Some like it hot, some like it cold,
Some like it in the pot, nine days old.

# THIS LITTLE PIGGY

This little piggy went to market,
This little piggy stayed home,
This little piggy had roast beef,
This little piggy had none,
And this little piggy cried,
"Wee-wee-wee-wee-wee,"
All the way home.

# ONE, TWO, BUCKLE MY SHOE

1, 2, buckle my shoe;
3, 4, shut the door;
5, 6, pick up sticks;
7, 8, lay them straight;
9, 10, a big fat hen;
11, 12, dig and delve;
13, 14, maids a-courting;
15, 16, maids in the kitchen;
17, 18, maids in waiting;
19, 20, my plate's empty.

# GOD IS GREAT

God is great, God is good,
Let us thank Him for this food.
By his hands we all are fed,
Give us, Lord, our daily bread.


# THANK YOU

Thank you for the world so sweet,
Thank you for the food we eat.
Thank you for the birds that sing,
Thank you, God, for everything.

# LITTLE DROPS OF WATER

Little drops of water,
Little grains of sand,
Make the mighty ocean,
And the pleasant land.

Little deeds of kindness,
Little words of love,
Help to make earth happy,
Like the heaven above.

# MAGIC WORDS

Hearts, like doors, will open with ease
To very, very little keys.
And don't forget that three of these
Are "Thank you," "You're welcome," and
 "If you please."

# MY SHADOW

I have a little shadow that
   goes in and out with me,
And what can be the use of him
   is more than I can see.
He is very, very like me
   from the heels up to the head;
And I see him jump before me,
   when I jump into my bed.

               *–Robert Louis Stevenson*

# LITTLE FOLKS

Little folks, little folks,
Now then for bed!
A pillow is waiting
For each little head.

Sleep all the night
And wake in the morn,
When early I sound
The call on my horn.

## THE MOON

I see the moon,
And the moon sees me;
God bless the moon,
And God bless me!

## STAR WISH

Star light, star bright,
First star I see tonight,
I wish I may, I wish I might,
Have the wish I wish tonight.

## WE GIVE OUR THANKS

We give our thanks to Thee today,
For Thou hast blessed us in every way.
Help us to do the things we should,
To be to others kind and good.

## NOW I LAY ME DOWN TO SLEEP

Now I lay me down to sleep,
I pray Thee, Lord, my soul to keep;
Thy love stay with me through the night
And wake me with the morning light.

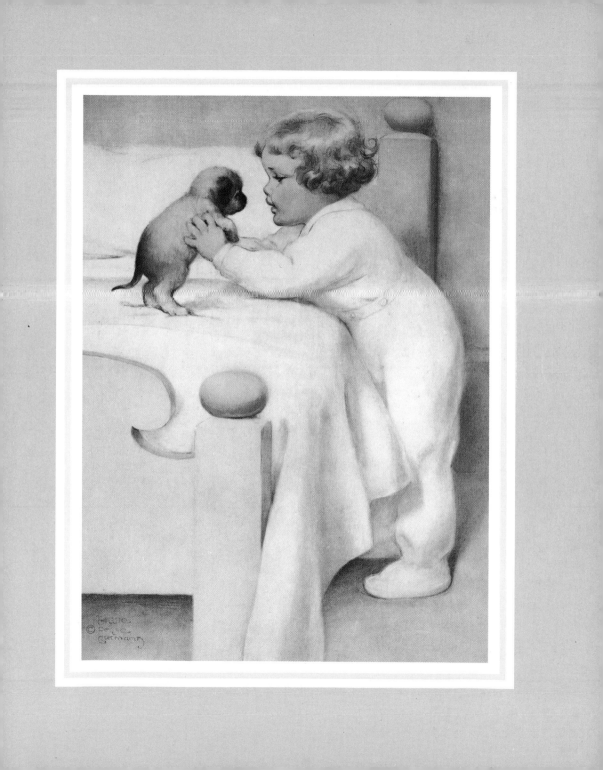

# GOOD NIGHT

Good night! Good night!
Far flies the light;
But still God's love
Shall flame above,
Making all bright.
Good night! Good night!

–Victor Hugo